Democracy for Sale

The Rise of
Plutocratic Capitalism
in the USA

A Short Introduction by K.R. Stonebridge

Democracy for Sale:
The Rise of Plutocratic Capitalism in the USA

ISBN: 9798877556218

Copyright © 2024 Brevity Books

Printed in the United States of America

Contents

Chapter 6:
Pathways to Reform

Chapter 7:
Envisioning a New Future

Chapter 1:
The Roots of
Plutocratic Capitalism

The Birth of Capitalism in America

In exploring the origins of capitalism in the United States, it's crucial to understand how this economic system took root and evolved in a landscape primarily shaped by democratic values. The birth of American capitalism is a story interwoven with the nation's very foundation, reflecting both its pioneering spirit and its early confrontations with the complex interplay of wealth and power.

In the nascent stages of American history, capitalism emerged not just as an economic system but as a cultural force. The early American economy was characterized by a spirit of entrepreneurship and a strong belief in individualism. This environment provided fertile ground for capitalism to grow. The doctrine of 'Manifest Destiny' and the westward expansion epitomized this spirit, linking economic growth with national destiny. However, as the nation expanded, so too did the complexities of its economic system, laying a foundation for disparities in wealth and power.

The Industrial Revolution marked a significant turning point. The transformation from agrarian economies to industrial production changed not just the economic landscape but also the social fabric of the country. The rise of industrial magnates, often termed as the 'Robber Barons', underscored a growing divide between the wealthy elite and the working class. This era witnessed the first major consolidation of wealth and the emergence of monopolies, setting the stage for future conflicts between democratic ideals and capitalist realities.

Simultaneously, the concept of the 'American Dream' began to take shape, rooted in the belief that anyone, regardless of their background, could achieve success through hard work. This belief was integral to the acceptance and propagation of capitalism. However, as the 20th century progressed, the realities of this dream began to diverge significantly from its idealized version. The Great Depression, in particular, highlighted the vulnerabilities of an unregulated capitalist system and led to significant governmental interventions designed to protect the common citizen, such as the New Deal.

The post-World War II era marked another significant phase, characterized by a booming economy and a growing middle class. However, it also witnessed the beginning of a gradual shift towards what we now recognize as plutocratic capitalism. Economic policies increasingly favored the wealthy, leading to a significant concentration of wealth. The deregulation of industries and the weakening of labor unions further exacerbated this trend, contributing to growing income inequality.

The late 20th and early 21st centuries have seen the culmination of these trends, with the increasing influence of corporate money in politics, the rise of lobbying, and the advent of the Citizen's United decision, further blurring the lines between economic and political power. The result is a form of capitalism that has strayed far from its early roots, where wealth not only generates more wealth but also translates into political influence.

In examining the birth of capitalism in America, it's evident that the system's evolution has been shaped by a constant tension between democratic ideals and economic realities. The early seeds of entrepreneurship and individualism have, over centuries, grown into a tree whose branches now cast a shadow over the very principles upon which the nation was founded. Understanding this historical context is crucial to comprehending the current state of American plutocracy and the challenges it poses to the country's democratic foundations.

Wealth Accumulation and Political Power

The intertwining of wealth accumulation and political power in the United States represents a critical dimension of how plutocratic capitalism has come to dominate the American socio-political landscape. This section delves into the historical and contemporary facets of this entanglement, exploring how concentrated wealth has progressively translated into significant political influence, thereby reshaping the democratic framework of the nation.

Historically, the accumulation of wealth in America has always been closely tied to political power. Post-Independence, landowners and industrial magnates wielded significant influence, often directly involved in political decision-making. The Gilded Age, in particular, epitomizes this phenomenon, where figures like John D. Rockefeller and Andrew Carnegie dominated not just the economy but also wielded considerable political influence. The monopolistic practices of this era and the political clout of the magnates led to public outcry and subsequent regulatory efforts, such as the Sherman Antitrust Act. However, these early attempts at regulation were often limited in their effectiveness.

In the 20th century, the nexus of wealth and politics took on new dimensions. The advent of modern financial systems and the rise of corporate power led to a more sophisticated interaction between economic and political spheres. Lobbying emerged as a formalized avenue for private interests to influence public policy. The influence was not always overt; it often operated through the funding of political campaigns, shaping of public opinion via media control, and the revolving door between corporate positions and government roles.

The latter half of the 20th century saw a significant shift with the relaxation of regulations and the rise of neoliberal economic policies. This period marked a substantial increase in the concentration of wealth, particularly among the top 1% of the population. The deregulation of various sectors, including finance and telecommunications, further empowered corporate entities. This economic power directly translated into political influence, with corporations and wealthy individuals increasingly shaping policy decisions, ranging from tax laws to environmental regulations.

The landmark Supreme Court decision in Citizens United v. Federal Election Commission in 2010 further exacerbated this situation. By allowing unlimited corporate spending in elections, it gave rise to Super PACs and dark money in politics, further obscuring the sources and influence of campaign financing. This decision effectively elevated the role of wealth in American politics, allowing those with financial resources to have a disproportionate impact on elections and policy-making.

In contemporary America, the implications of this wealth-politics nexus are profound. Economic policies increasingly favor the wealthy, contributing to a cycle where wealth begets more wealth, and in turn, more political influence. This cycle poses a significant challenge to the principles of egalitarian democracy, as the voices of ordinary citizens are marginalized in the political process. Policy decisions tend to align more closely with the interests of the wealthy elite, often at the expense of broader societal needs. This disparity has led to growing public discontent and questions about the integrity of American democracy.

Furthermore, the influence of wealth in politics has implications for a range of issues, from income inequality to climate change. Policies that could address these issues are often stalled or diluted due to the influence of wealthy interest groups. For instance, significant action on climate change is frequently impeded by the fossil fuel lobby, despite widespread public support for environmental protection.

The accumulation of wealth and its translation into political power is a defining feature of American plutocracy. It challenges the foundational democratic principle that political power should stem from the people rather than from financial influence. Understanding this dynamic is crucial to comprehending the current state of American democracy and the potential paths for reform.

The Shifting Landscape: From Democracy to Plutocracy

The transition from democracy to plutocracy in the United States is a complex and multifaceted process, representing a gradual but significant shift in the balance of power from the broader populace to a wealthy elite. This section examines the various factors and events that have contributed to this transformation, highlighting the erosion of democratic principles and the rise of plutocratic influence in American society.

The concept of democracy in America has been traditionally rooted in the ideals of equal representation and the notion that the government should reflect the will of the people. However, the increasing influence of money in politics and the concentration of wealth have gradually eroded these foundational principles. The shift towards plutocracy–a system where the wealthy hold disproportionate power and influence–has been gradual but unmistakable.

One of the critical drivers of this shift has been the changing economic landscape. Over the past few decades, the United States has seen a dramatic rise in income and wealth inequality. The top one percent of the population has accumulated a disproportionate share of the nation's wealth, while wage stagnation and growing living costs have left the middle and lower classes increasingly vulnerable. This economic divide has created a power imbalance, where the wealthy have both the means and the motivation to influence political outcomes in their favor.

The role of money in politics has been a significant factor in this transition. Campaign financing, particularly in the wake of decisions like Citizens United v. FEC, has allowed unprecedented amounts of private wealth to flow into the political arena. This influx of money has not only skewed the electoral process but has also led to a situation where elected officials are often more responsive to the interests of their wealthy donors than to the needs of their constituents. The result is a political system that is increasingly disconnected from the average voter, with policies that often favor the wealthy at the expense of the broader public good.

Another contributing factor is the lobbying industry. The growth of lobbying efforts, both in terms of money spent and the number of lobbyists, has given special interest groups, often representing wealthy entities, significant sway over legislation and policy-making. This influence is not always transparent, making it difficult for the average citizen to understand or counteract.

The media landscape has also played a role in this shift. The consolidation of media ownership into the hands of a few wealthy corporations has led to a homogenization of perspectives, often aligning with corporate interests. This concentration of media power not only shapes public opinion but also determines the issues and viewpoints that receive attention, further marginalizing alternative perspectives and grassroots movements.

The erosion of democratic institutions has been both a cause and a consequence of the rise of plutocracy. Gerrymandering, voter suppression tactics, and the weakening of labor unions are examples of how democratic processes have been manipulated to maintain the status quo of wealth and power concentration. These practices undermine the principles of fair representation and equal participation, essential tenets of a functioning democracy.

The shift from democracy to plutocracy is not merely a political issue; it has profound social implications. It exacerbates social divisions, undermines public trust in institutions, and stifles social mobility. The disillusionment and disenfranchisement of large segments of the population can lead to social unrest and a weakening of the social fabric that holds the nation together.

In conclusion, the transformation of the United States from a democracy to a plutocracy has been a gradual but steady process, driven by economic inequality, the influence of money in politics, lobbying, media consolidation, and the erosion of democratic institutions. This shift poses a significant challenge to the ideals of equal representation and government by the people. Understanding and addressing the root causes of this transformation are crucial to restoring democratic principles and ensuring that the government serves the interests of all its citizens, not just a wealthy few.

Chapter 2:
The Mechanics of Power

Lobbying and Political Influence

The landscape of American politics is significantly shaped by the dynamics of lobbying and political influence. This relationship, central to understanding plutocratic capitalism, reveals how powerful interest groups, often representing wealthy entities, exert considerable sway over the legislative and policy-making processes in the United States. In this section, we delve into the mechanisms of lobbying, its evolution, and its profound impact on American democracy.

Lobbying, in its essence, is the act of attempting to influence decisions made by officials in the government, most often legislators or members of regulatory agencies. While lobbying is a legitimate and constitutionally protected activity, essential for the representation of diverse interests in a democracy, its current form and scale in the United States have raised concerns about the integrity and inclusiveness of the democratic process.

Historically, lobbying in America has roots in the early days of the republic, but it has grown exponentially in both scope and complexity in the modern era. The last few decades have seen a dramatic increase in the amount of money spent on lobbying, paralleled by a surge in the number of lobbyists operating in Washington, D.C., and across state capitals. This growth is attributed to the increasing realization among various sectors that government decisions can have a substantial impact on their interests.

The nature of lobbying has evolved to include not just direct interactions with policymakers but also a broader range of activities like funding research, organizing public relations campaigns, and mobilizing public opinion. Lobbyists today are often professionals with expertise in specific policy areas, equipped to navigate the intricacies of legislative and regulatory processes. They play a key role in drafting legislation, providing data and arguments to policymakers, and shaping the public narrative around key issues.

One of the critical concerns about lobbying is the disproportionate influence it affords to wealthy individuals and corporations. The high cost of effective lobbying efforts means that these activities are more accessible to entities with significant financial resources. As a result, the interests and perspectives of these entities are often more prominently represented and heard in the halls of power, compared to those of ordinary citizens or less affluent groups.

The impact of lobbying on the democratic process is profound and multifaceted. On a legislative level, there is evidence to suggest that lobbying efforts can significantly influence the likelihood of bills being passed, the content of legislation, and the priorities of lawmakers. This influence often aligns with the interests of the lobbying entities, which may not always coincide with the broader public interest or democratic ideals.

Moreover, the prevalence of lobbying can lead to a form of policy capture, where regulatory and legislative decisions are disproportionately shaped by the interests of the most powerful lobbying groups. This situation can lead to the creation of policies that reinforce existing power structures and economic inequalities, further entrenching plutocratic capitalism.

The relationship between lobbyists and policymakers also raises ethical concerns. The revolving door phenomenon, where individuals move between positions in government and lobbying firms, can lead to conflicts of interest and a blurring of the lines between public service and private gain. This practice can undermine public trust in government institutions and fuel perceptions of corruption.

In response to these concerns, there have been calls for reforming the lobbying system in the United States. Proposals include stricter disclosure requirements, limits on lobbying expenditures, and restrictions on the revolving door between government positions and lobbying firms. However, implementing these reforms has been challenging, partly due to the very influence of powerful lobbying groups that would be affected by such changes.

In summary, lobbying and political influence play a critical role in shaping the mechanics of power in the United States. While lobbying is a necessary component of a democratic system, its current scale and nature in the American context raise significant concerns about the balance of interests and the integrity of democratic processes. Addressing these concerns is crucial for ensuring that the political system serves the broader public interest and upholds democratic values.

The Role of Campaign Finance

Campaign finance, an integral aspect of the American political system, plays a pivotal role in shaping the dynamics of power and influence. This section delves into the complexities of campaign financing in the United States, examining how it affects the democratic process and contributes to the entrenchment of plutocratic capitalism.

The financing of political campaigns in the U.S. has evolved into a system where significant funds are required to run competitive campaigns, especially for high-profile offices like the presidency or congressional seats. This necessity for substantial financial backing fundamentally impacts who can viably run for office, what policies are promoted, and whose interests are prioritized in the political arena.

The roots of the current campaign finance system can be traced back to various legislative acts and court decisions. Key among these is the Bipartisan Campaign Reform Act (BCRA) of 2002, also known as the McCain-Feingold Act, which aimed to regulate the financing of political campaigns. However, the landscape of campaign finance was dramatically altered by the Supreme Court's 2010 decision in Citizens United v. Federal Election Commission. This ruling, and subsequent decisions like McCutcheon v. FEC, significantly deregulated campaign finance laws, allowing for unlimited spending by corporations, labor unions, and other groups in elections and leading to the proliferation of Super PACs (Political Action Committees).

These developments have had profound implications for American democracy. The influx of vast sums of money into politics has intensified concerns about the influence of wealthy donors and special interest groups. Candidates often rely on contributions from a small segment of wealthy individuals and corporations, potentially leading to a scenario where elected officials are more responsive to these donors than to the average voter.

The role of money in elections also impacts the nature of political discourse and campaigning. Campaigns increasingly focus on fundraising and catering to the interests of large donors. This dynamic can lead to a narrow policy focus, overlooking broader societal concerns that may not align with the interests of wealthy contributors. Additionally, the need for substantial funding can discourage potential candidates who lack access to wealthy donors, effectively narrowing the pool of individuals who can realistically pursue political office.

Another aspect of campaign finance that raises concerns is the lack of transparency in some funding sources. The rise of "dark money" – funds from donors who are not legally required to disclose their identities – obscures the true source of campaign contributions, making it difficult for voters to understand who is influencing candidates and elections.

The impact of the current campaign finance system extends beyond elections; it influences policymaking and governance. Elected officials, aware of the need to finance future campaigns, may be inclined to support policies favorable to their donors, further perpetuating a cycle where money wields significant influence over political decisions.

In response to these challenges, there have been various efforts at reforming campaign finance, aiming to reduce the influence of money in politics and restore a more egalitarian democratic process. These efforts include calls for public financing of campaigns, stricter disclosure requirements for donors, and limits on campaign spending. However, implementing such reforms faces significant challenges, not least because of the entrenched interests that benefit from the current system.

In summary, the role of campaign finance in the United States is a critical factor in understanding the mechanics of power within the political system. The necessity for substantial financial resources in campaigns has created a landscape where wealth and influence are increasingly intertwined, challenging the principles of democratic representation and equality. Addressing the complexities of campaign finance is essential for ensuring a more balanced and representative political system that truly reflects the will of the American people.

Media Manipulation and Public Opinion

In the intricate tapestry of American politics, media manipulation and its influence on public opinion are pivotal elements. This section explores how media, in its various forms, has been utilized to shape public perception and opinion, furthering the interests of those in power and contributing to the entrenchment of plutocratic capitalism in the United States.

The media, often termed the "fourth estate," plays a critical role in a democracy, providing information, shaping public discourse, and acting as a watchdog against abuses of power. However, in the context of plutocratic capitalism, the media has also been used as a tool for manipulating public opinion to serve specific interests, particularly those of the wealthy and powerful.

One of the key ways this manipulation occurs is through the ownership and control of media outlets. The consolidation of media companies in the hands of a few large corporations has resulted in a homogenization of viewpoints and a narrowing of the information presented to the public. These media conglomerates often have their own political and economic interests, which can influence the content they produce and distribute. This concentration of media power limits the diversity of perspectives and can skew public understanding of important issues.

Another aspect of media manipulation is the strategic use of news and information to shape public opinion. This can involve the selective presentation of facts, the framing of stories to reflect a particular viewpoint, or the omission of information that contradicts desired narratives. Such tactics can subtly influence public perception and opinion, often without overtly appearing biased or manipulative.

The advent of social media and digital platforms has added another dimension to this dynamic. While these platforms have democratized content creation and distribution, allowing for a wider range of voices and perspectives, they have also become tools for targeted influence campaigns. The use of algorithms, echo chambers, and filter bubbles can reinforce existing beliefs and opinions, making it challenging for individuals to access or consider alternative viewpoints.

In addition to shaping public opinion, media manipulation also plays a role in setting the political agenda. By choosing which issues to highlight and how to frame them, media outlets can influence what the public perceives as important or worthy of discussion. This power can be used to divert attention from critical issues, especially those that might threaten the interests of the wealthy elite.

The impact of media manipulation extends to electoral processes. Political advertising, particularly negative campaigning, has become a significant aspect of elections. Funded by large sums of money, often from anonymous sources, these ads can significantly influence voter perceptions and decisions. The lack of transparency and regulation around such advertising further exacerbates its impact on democratic processes.

The consequences of media manipulation for democracy are profound. When public opinion is shaped by a media landscape that is not representative of the broader population, it can lead to policies and political outcomes that favor a minority of wealthy and powerful interests. This situation undermines the democratic principle that government should reflect the will of the people.

Addressing the challenges posed by media manipulation requires a multifaceted approach. This could include promoting media literacy among the public, ensuring greater diversity in media ownership, enforcing transparency in political advertising, and regulating digital platforms to mitigate the spread of misinformation. Such measures can help create a media environment that supports a healthy and representative democratic process.

In conclusion, the manipulation of media and its influence on public opinion is a critical aspect of the power dynamics in American politics. It highlights the challenges faced by a democracy when information and discourse are controlled or influenced by a few powerful entities. Addressing these challenges is crucial for ensuring that the media serves its role as a pillar of democracy, facilitating informed public discourse and holding power to account.

Chapter 3: Case Studies of Plutocratic Influence

Wall Street and the Financial Sector

The relationship between Wall Street and the political landscape of the United States epitomizes the intricate interplay between economic power and political influence. This section explores how the financial sector, particularly Wall Street, has exerted significant influence over American economic policies and political decisions, illustrating the practical workings of plutocratic capitalism.

Wall Street, as a symbol and physical embodiment of the American financial sector, wields considerable influence in the corridors of power in Washington, D.C. This influence is not merely a by-product of the sector's economic significance but is also a result of deliberate strategies employed to shape policy and regulatory environments favorable to its interests.

The financial sector's power in shaping economic policy can be traced back to various historical milestones. The deregulation wave of the 1980s and 1990s, for instance, removed many of the constraints imposed on the financial industry in the aftermath of the Great Depression. These policy shifts, championed by Wall Street, were predicated on the belief that free markets and limited government intervention would lead to greater efficiency and economic growth. However, this era of deregulation also set the stage for increased financial speculation and risk-taking, culminating in the 2008 financial crisis.

The 2008 crisis was a pivotal moment in illustrating the relationship between Wall Street and political power. The response to the crisis, particularly the government's decision to bail out major financial institutions deemed "too big to fail," highlighted the sector's influence. The rationale for these bailouts was rooted in the fear of systemic collapse, but they also raised questions about moral hazard and the preferential treatment of financial elites at the expense of ordinary taxpayers.

Lobbying and campaign contributions have been key tools for Wall Street to exert its influence. The financial sector is one of the largest sources of political donations in the United States, funding campaigns across the political spectrum. This financial support gives the sector leverage in shaping legislation and regulatory decisions. For instance, the Dodd-Frank Wall Street Reform and Consumer Protection Act, passed in response to the 2008 crisis, was subject to intense lobbying by financial institutions, which succeeded in watering down some of its provisions.

Another aspect of Wall Street's influence is evident in the revolving door between the financial sector and government. Many high-ranking government officials, including Treasury Secretaries and economic advisors, have come directly from or returned to positions in major financial institutions. This interchange raises concerns about conflicts of interest and the alignment of economic policies with the interests of the financial elite.

The impact of Wall Street's influence extends beyond specific policies and into broader economic and societal implications. The sector's prioritization of short-term profits, often at the expense of long-term stability and equitable growth, has contributed to economic disparities and social tensions. The increasing financialization of the economy, where profits are increasingly derived from financial activities rather than productive enterprises, has also been linked to rising inequality and the erosion of the middle class.

In response to these challenges, there have been calls for stricter regulation of the financial sector, greater transparency in political contributions, and reforms to reduce the revolving door phenomenon. Proposals for more robust financial regulation aim to balance the sector's role in economic growth with the need to protect against systemic risks and ensure fairness.

In conclusion, Wall Street and the financial sector's influence over American politics and policy decisions is a clear example of how economic power can translate into political power. This influence not only shapes economic policies but also has significant implications for democratic governance and social equity. Addressing the challenges posed by this influence is essential for ensuring a more balanced economic system and a healthier democratic process.

Big Tech and Information Control

The ascendancy of Big Tech companies has introduced a new dynamic in the landscape of plutocratic capitalism, particularly in their control over information and its dissemination. This section delves into the role of major technology companies in shaping public discourse, their influence on political processes, and the challenges they pose to democratic principles in the United States.

The rise of Big Tech – companies like Google, Facebook, Amazon, and Apple – has been meteoric, driven by rapid advancements in technology and the increasing digitization of society. These companies have revolutionized how information is accessed, consumed, and shared, effectively becoming gatekeepers of digital communication and information flow. While they have brought undeniable benefits in terms of connectivity and access to information, their outsized influence and control over the digital landscape have raised significant concerns.

One of the primary issues is the concentration of power in the hands of a few large tech companies. Their platforms are not just conduits for information but also shape the nature and distribution of content. Algorithms determine what news and opinions are seen by whom, often based on engagement metrics that prioritize sensational or divisive content. This algorithmic curation can create echo chambers and filter bubbles, reinforcing existing beliefs and biases, and potentially distorting the public's understanding of key issues.

Big Tech's role in political processes has come under intense scrutiny. Social media platforms have become crucial arenas for political discourse, campaigning, and the mobilization of public opinion. However, the spread of misinformation and the use of these platforms for political manipulation – as seen in various election interference scandals – have highlighted the challenges in ensuring fair and transparent political processes in the digital age.

The economic power of Big Tech also translates into significant political influence. These companies are among the biggest spenders on lobbying in Washington, D.C., seeking to shape policies and regulations in areas like privacy, antitrust, and taxation. Their financial clout gives them considerable sway over legislative outcomes, raising questions about the balance of interests in the policymaking process.

Another aspect of Big Tech's influence is their role in the broader economy. Their dominance in certain sectors, often achieved through aggressive growth strategies and the acquisition of potential competitors, has raised antitrust concerns. There are fears that such market dominance not only stifles competition but also concentrates economic power in ways that can be detrimental to consumers, innovation, and the economy as a whole.

The power of Big Tech companies extends to the workplace and labor market. Their practices, from gig economy models to the treatment of workers, set trends that other industries follow. The debate over these practices often reflects broader societal concerns about workers' rights, income inequality, and the future of work in an increasingly digital economy.

In response to these challenges, there have been growing calls for regulating Big Tech, with proposals ranging from antitrust action to the regulation of online content. The debate over how to balance the benefits of technology with the need to curb the excesses of these powerful corporations is a complex one, involving issues of free speech, innovation, privacy, and market competition.

In conclusion, the influence of Big Tech in the realm of information control and their broader role in society exemplifies the complexities of modern plutocratic capitalism. Their ability to shape public discourse, influence political processes, and dominate key economic sectors poses significant challenges to democratic governance and fair market competition. Addressing these challenges requires thoughtful and balanced approaches, ensuring that the digital landscape supports democratic values and equitable economic growth.

The Fossil Fuel Industry and Environmental Policy

The fossil fuel industry's influence on environmental policy in the United States is a striking example of how plutocratic interests can shape critical aspects of governance and public policy. This section examines the ways in which the coal, oil, and natural gas industries have exerted their power to affect environmental regulations, climate change policies, and the broader discourse on sustainable development.

Historically, the fossil fuel industry has been a cornerstone of the American economy. Its development has been closely tied to the nation's growth and has played a central role in shaping economic policy. However, as scientific understanding of climate change has evolved, revealing the significant impact of fossil fuels on global warming and environmental degradation, the industry has found itself at the center of a contentious debate over environmental policy.

One of the primary ways the fossil fuel industry has exerted influence is through political lobbying and campaign contributions. The industry invests heavily in political campaigns and lobbying efforts, aiming to shape legislation and regulation in ways that protect its interests. This financial influence has been instrumental in shaping environmental policies, often slowing the adoption of stricter regulations on emissions and undermining efforts to transition to renewable energy sources.

The industry's influence extends to the public discourse on climate change and environmental policy. Through funding research and advocacy groups, the fossil fuel industry has been involved in efforts to question the scientific consensus on climate change, amplify uncertainties, and downplay the urgency of environmental action. These strategies have contributed to a polarized public debate, making it more challenging to achieve consensus on environmental policies.

Regulatory capture is another aspect of the industry's influence. This phenomenon occurs when regulatory agencies, established to act in the public interest, become dominated by the industries they are supposed to regulate. In the case of the fossil fuel industry, there have been instances where regulatory bodies have been staffed by former industry executives or have been subject to intense lobbying, leading to policies and decisions that favor industry interests over environmental protection.

The impact of the fossil fuel industry's influence on environmental policy is profound. It has implications for national and global efforts to address climate change, air and water quality, and public health. Policies that favor the continued use of fossil fuels not only contribute to environmental degradation but also hinder the development and adoption of cleaner and more sustainable energy technologies.

The industry's influence also affects international policies and agreements. The United States, as a major global emitter and a leader in energy production, plays a significant role in international climate negotiations. The stance and policies of the U.S. government, often influenced by the fossil fuel industry, can have far-reaching consequences for global climate action and cooperation.

In response to these challenges, there have been growing calls for more stringent regulation of the fossil fuel industry, increased transparency in lobbying and campaign finance, and greater investment in renewable energy. Advocates for environmental reform argue that mitigating the influence of the fossil fuel industry is essential for addressing climate change and transitioning to a sustainable energy future.

In conclusion, the influence of the fossil fuel industry on environmental policy in the United States highlights the complex interplay between economic interests and public policy. The industry's ability to shape legislative, regulatory, and public discourse on environmental issues illustrates the challenges faced in aligning economic activities with sustainable and equitable development. Addressing these challenges requires a concerted effort to balance economic interests with the urgent need for environmental stewardship and climate action.

Chapter 4: Societal Impact

Widening Economic Inequality

The issue of widening economic inequality in the United States is a critical societal impact of plutocratic capitalism. This section explores the dimensions and drivers of this growing disparity, its implications for society, and the role of policy and economic structures in exacerbating or mitigating inequality.

Over the past few decades, economic inequality in the U.S. has reached levels not seen since the Gilded Age. This inequality manifests in various forms–income, wealth, opportunity, and access to essential services. The top fraction of the population has seen substantial increases in their wealth and income, while the middle and lower economic classes have faced stagnation and, in many cases, a decline in their financial well-being.

Several factors contribute to this widening economic divide. One significant driver is the changing nature of the economy and the labor market. Technological advancements and globalization have resulted in a shift in the types of jobs available, often favoring higher-skilled workers and leaving behind those in lower-skilled occupations. This shift has been accompanied by a decline in labor union power and a decrease in manufacturing jobs, which traditionally provided stable, middle-class incomes.

Tax policies and government regulations, or lack thereof, have also played a role in exacerbating inequality. Tax reforms, especially those favoring the wealthy and corporations, have contributed to the concentration of wealth. Simultaneously, deregulation in certain sectors has allowed for corporate practices that prioritize shareholder profits, often at the expense of worker wages and benefits.

The financialization of the economy is another contributing factor. This process, where economic growth is increasingly driven by financial activities rather than the production of goods and services, has resulted in wealth accumulation for those with assets and investments, widening the gap between them and those relying primarily on wages.

Inequality is not just an economic issue; it has profound societal implications. High levels of economic disparity can lead to reduced social mobility, creating a cycle where the disadvantaged remain so across generations. This situation undermines the foundational American belief in the "American Dream" – the idea that hard work and determination can lead to success, regardless of one's starting point in life.

Widening inequality also has repercussions for social cohesion and stability. It can lead to increased social tensions, erode trust in institutions, and fuel political polarization. The perception that the economic system is rigged in favor of the wealthy can lead to disillusionment and disenfranchisement among large segments of the population.

The health and well-being of individuals are also affected by economic inequality. Research has shown correlations between high levels of inequality and adverse health outcomes, including higher rates of mental illness, lower life expectancy, and increased incidence of chronic diseases. These health disparities are often exacerbated by unequal access to healthcare and other essential services.

Addressing economic inequality requires a multifaceted approach. Potential solutions include reforming tax policies to ensure a more equitable distribution of wealth, investing in education and workforce training to prepare workers for the changing economy, and strengthening social safety nets to support those in need. Additionally, policies promoting fair wages, affordable housing, and accessible healthcare can directly impact reducing inequality.

In conclusion, widening economic inequality is a significant societal impact of the current economic system in the United States.

It is a multifaceted issue, deeply intertwined with the structures
and policies of plutocratic capitalism. Tackling this challenge is
essential not only for economic reasons but for the health and
stability of American society as a whole.

Eroding Democratic Institutions

The erosion of democratic institutions in the United States is a
significant societal impact of plutocratic capitalism, where the consolidation of wealth and power in the hands of a few undermines
the democratic principles of equality and fair representation.
This section examines how plutocratic influences have led to the
weakening of democratic institutions and the implications of this
erosion for American society and governance.

Democratic institutions in the U.S. are foundational to its political system, designed to uphold the principles of representation,
accountability, and the rule of law. However, the influence of concentrated wealth and power has increasingly compromised these
institutions, threatening the democratic fabric of the nation.

One of the most apparent signs of this erosion is seen in the
electoral process. The influx of money into politics, especially
following the Citizens United v. FEC decision, has skewed the
democratic process. When political campaigns and candidates
depend heavily on funding from wealthy donors and corporations,
it raises questions about their independence and alignment with
the broader public interest. This dependency can lead to a system
where policies and decisions favor a small, affluent segment of the
population, rather than reflecting the collective will.

Gerrymandering, the practice of manipulating electoral district
boundaries to favor specific parties or groups, is another tactic that
undermines democratic institutions. By ensuring predetermined
electoral outcomes, gerrymandering distorts the principle of fair
representation, making it difficult for certain voices and perspectives to be heard in the political arena.

The erosion of democratic institutions is also evident in legislative gridlock and the declining efficacy of governance. When political decisions are heavily influenced by wealthy interests, it can lead to policies that serve those interests, even if they are at odds with the public good or democratic principles. This situation can result in a lack of meaningful progress on critical issues, diminishing public trust in government institutions.

Judicial independence is another cornerstone of democratic institutions that can be compromised by plutocratic influences. The politicization of judicial appointments, where judges are selected based on their alignment with certain economic or political interests, threatens the impartiality and integrity of the judiciary. A compromised judiciary can lead to legal decisions that protect the interests of the wealthy, further entrenching plutocratic power.

The erosion of democratic institutions extends beyond formal political structures to encompass the broader public sphere. The weakening of a free and independent press, essential for holding power to account, is a concern. Media consolidation and the influence of wealthy owners can lead to biased reporting and a lack of diverse perspectives, limiting the public's ability to make informed decisions.

The implications of this erosion are profound. A weakened democratic system can lead to increased social and economic inequality, as policies favor the interests of a few over the needs of the many. It can also result in reduced civic engagement and political participation, as citizens feel disillusioned and powerless to effect change.

Furthermore, the undermining of democratic institutions can have global repercussions. The United States, as a leading democratic nation, sets an example for other countries. Erosion of its democratic principles can weaken the global push for democratic governance and human rights.

Addressing the erosion of democratic institutions requires a concerted effort to realign the political system with democratic ideals. This effort could include campaign finance reform, measures to ensure fair electoral processes, strengthening checks and balances, and promoting media diversity and independence. Engaging citizens in political processes and fostering a culture of transparency and accountability are also crucial for revitalizing democratic institutions.

In conclusion, the erosion of democratic institutions in the United States is a critical issue arising from the dominance of plutocratic capitalism. This erosion threatens the foundational principles of democracy, leading to governance that favors the few over the many. Addressing this challenge is essential for preserving the democratic character of the nation and ensuring that its institutions serve the public interest.

The Decline of Social Mobility

The decline of social mobility in the United States is a significant consequence of the widening economic inequality and the erosion of democratic institutions, both hallmarks of plutocratic capitalism. This section examines the factors contributing to the stagnation of social mobility, its implications for the American dream, and the broader societal impact.

Social mobility, the ability of individuals to move up the economic ladder within their lifetime or from one generation to the next, has long been a cornerstone of the American ethos. The United States has prided itself on being a land of opportunity, where hard work and ambition can lead to upward social and economic mobility regardless of one's starting point. However, in recent decades, this ideal has increasingly come under threat.

Several factors contribute to the decline in social mobility. One of the most significant is the growing income and wealth inequality. As the gap between the rich and the poor widens, it becomes increasingly difficult for individuals from lower-income brackets to break out of their economic circumstances. Wealthy families can afford to invest in education, health, and networking opportunities for their children, giving them a considerable advantage in the job market. In contrast, those from less affluent backgrounds often face barriers to accessing quality education and career opportunities.

Another contributing factor is the changing nature of the economy and the job market. The shift toward a knowledge-based economy has placed a premium on higher education and specialized skills. However, the rising cost of higher education and the burden of student debt have made it increasingly difficult for individuals from lower-income families to obtain the qualifications needed for upward mobility.

Housing plays a crucial role in social mobility. The increasing cost of living in areas with good schools and job opportunities has made it difficult for lower-income families to access these critical resources. Additionally, zoning laws and housing policies in many parts of the country have reinforced socioeconomic segregation, further entrenching inequality.

The weakening of social safety nets and public institutions that traditionally provided pathways to upward mobility is another factor. Cuts to public education, healthcare, and social services have disproportionately affected those at the lower end of the economic spectrum, limiting their opportunities for advancement.

The implications of declining social mobility are far-reaching. It challenges the foundational narrative of the American dream, leading to disillusionment and a sense of injustice, particularly among younger generations. This disillusionment can foster social and political discontent, contributing to polarization and instability.

Declining social mobility also has economic implications. When a significant portion of the population is unable to reach its full economic potential, it leads to a waste of human capital and a drag on economic growth. Moreover, a lack of mobility can stifle innovation and entrepreneurship, as individuals from lower-income backgrounds may not have the resources or opportunities to pursue new ideas and business ventures.

Addressing the decline in social mobility requires a comprehensive approach that tackles the underlying factors of economic inequality and systemic barriers. This approach could include policies aimed at reducing income and wealth inequality, such as progressive taxation and wealth redistribution measures. Investing in education, affordable housing, and healthcare is crucial to providing equal opportunities for all.

Strengthening labor rights and protections can also play a role in promoting social mobility. Policies that support fair wages, worker benefits, and the right to unionize can help ensure that economic growth translates into improved opportunities and living standards for the broader population.

In conclusion, the decline of social mobility in the United States is a worrying trend that undermines the core values of the American dream. It reflects the deeper issues of economic inequality and eroding democratic institutions associated with plutocratic capitalism. Addressing this decline is essential not only for the sake of fairness and social justice but also for the health and vitality of American society and its economy.

Chapter 5:
Global Implications

International Economic Dominance

The international economic dominance of the United States, a central aspect of its global influence, is intricately connected to the dynamics of plutocratic capitalism. This section examines how the U.S.'s economic power shapes international relations, impacts global economic structures, and influences the economic policies of other nations.

Since the mid-20th century, the United States has been a dominant force in the global economy. This position has been underpinned by its substantial economic output, technological innovation, and the role of the U.S. dollar as the world's primary reserve currency. However, the nature of this dominance is deeply intertwined with the principles and practices of plutocratic capitalism, which have significant implications for the global economic landscape.

One of the key aspects of U.S. international economic dominance is its influence over global financial systems and institutions. The U.S. exerts considerable influence in international bodies such as the International Monetary Fund (IMF), the World Bank, and the World Trade Organization (WTO). Through these institutions, the U.S. has been able to shape global economic policies and standards, often in ways that reflect its own economic interests and those of its corporate sector. This influence has been instrumental in promoting free-market capitalism and liberalized trade policies worldwide.

The U.S.'s economic dominance also manifests in its role as a primary driver of global economic trends. American consumer markets, investment flows, and monetary policy have significant ripple effects across the global economy. For instance, decisions by the Federal Reserve on interest rates not only impact the U.S. economy but also have profound implications for emerging markets and global financial stability.

Another dimension of U.S. economic dominance is its role in setting technological and corporate standards. American technology companies and their platforms have become integral to the global digital economy, shaping how people worldwide communicate, access information, and conduct business. The dominance of these companies raises questions about data privacy, digital sovereignty, and the concentration of economic power in the hands of a few global corporations.

The U.S.'s approach to international trade and economic relations has also been a critical aspect of its dominance. Through trade agreements and economic partnerships, the U.S. has promoted the expansion of free trade and open markets. However, these policies have sometimes been critiqued for prioritizing the interests of American corporations and neglecting concerns about labor rights, environmental standards, and economic inequality.

The global influence of U.S. economic policies is not without its challenges and criticisms. The promotion of neoliberal economic policies, often associated with plutocratic capitalism, has been linked to issues such as income inequality, environmental degradation, and the erosion of social safety nets in various countries. Additionally, the U.S.'s stance on issues like climate change and international tax regulations has significant implications for global efforts to address these pressing challenges.

In recent years, there has been a growing debate about the sustainability of U.S. international economic dominance. Concerns about the long-term effects of income inequality, the concentration of corporate power, and the potential for economic and financial crises have prompted discussions about the need for a more balanced and equitable global economic order.

In conclusion, the international economic dominance of the United States, shaped by the principles of plutocratic capitalism, plays a pivotal role in the global economic landscape. This dominance impacts international economic policies, shapes global markets, and influences the economic trajectories of other nations. While it has contributed to the spread of free-market capitalism and technological innovation, it also poses challenges related to economic inequality, sustainability, and the need for a more equitable global economic system.

The Spread of Plutocratic Ideals

The spread of plutocratic ideals, influenced significantly by the economic and political practices of the United States, is a phenomenon with far-reaching global implications. This section explores how the principles of plutocratic capitalism, originating in the U.S., have permeated various aspects of global governance, economies, and societies, reshaping the world's approach to democracy, economic policy, and social welfare.

Plutocracy, the governance by the wealthy, has become an increasingly visible aspect of global political and economic systems. The U.S., with its blend of immense wealth, corporate power, and political influence, has been both a model and a catalyst for the spread of plutocratic ideals. This influence is evident in several key areas, including the global economy, international politics, and cultural values.

In the realm of the global economy, American-style capitalism, characterized by market liberalization, deregulation, and privatization, has been widely adopted. International financial institutions, often influenced by the U.S., have propagated these ideals, advocating for policies that favor open markets and private enterprise. While these policies have driven economic growth and expanded global trade, they have also been associated with increasing income inequality, reduced labor protections, and environmental degradation.

The political influence of wealth, a hallmark of plutocracy, has also become a global phenomenon. In many countries, the role of money in politics has grown, mirroring trends in the U.S. This development has led to concerns about the erosion of democratic processes, where electoral and policy outcomes are increasingly influenced by wealthy individuals and corporate interests rather than the electorate at large.

Culturally, the American dream, with its emphasis on individual success and wealth accumulation, has been an influential narrative, shaping societal values and aspirations around the world. The glorification of wealth and success, often portrayed in global media and popular culture, has contributed to a shift in values, prioritizing material wealth and consumption over social and communal goals.

However, the spread of plutocratic ideals has not been without resistance. Critiques of American-style capitalism have emerged, focusing on its sustainability, its social costs, and its impact on democratic governance. Movements advocating for greater income equality, corporate accountability, and the protection of social and environmental standards have gained traction globally.

In developing countries, the adoption of plutocratic policies has often led to complex challenges. While market liberalization has propelled economic growth in some cases, it has also resulted in increased inequality, exploitation of labor, and environmental harm. The promise of economic prosperity has often come at the cost of social and environmental well-being.

The spread of plutocratic ideals has also influenced international relations. The global dominance of the U.S. and its economic model has sometimes led to tensions, particularly in regions seeking to maintain their economic sovereignty and cultural identity. The balance of power, both economically and politically, is a continuing source of global dynamics and negotiations.

Moreover, the digital revolution, led by American tech giants, has brought new dimensions to the spread of plutocracy. The control over data, information, and digital infrastructure by a few corporations has raised questions about privacy, digital rights, and the concentration of power in the digital age.

In conclusion, the spread of plutocratic ideals, heavily influenced by the economic and political practices of the United States, has had a profound impact on the global landscape. While it has driven economic growth and global integration, it has also raised significant challenges related to inequality, democratic governance, and social welfare. Understanding and addressing these challenges is crucial for forging a path towards a more equitable and sustainable global order.

Global Responses and Resistance

The global spread of plutocratic ideals, originating largely from the United States, has not gone unchallenged. Around the world, there have been varied responses and forms of resistance to the encroachment of plutocratic capitalism, reflecting a complex tapestry of global dynamics. This section explores these global responses, highlighting the efforts to counteract or mitigate the influence of plutocracy in different regions and contexts.

Resistance to plutocratic capitalism has manifested in various forms, ranging from government policies and international agreements to grassroots movements and advocacy campaigns. These responses often arise from concerns about income inequality, environmental degradation, cultural erosion, and the loss of political sovereignty.

One significant form of resistance has been through policy and legislative changes at the national and international levels. Some countries have implemented measures aimed at curbing the influence of wealth in politics, strengthening labor rights, and enhancing social welfare systems. These efforts are often driven by a desire to maintain economic sovereignty, protect cultural identities, and ensure more equitable growth. For instance, several European nations have adopted progressive taxation systems, robust social safety nets, and strict campaign finance laws to mitigate the effects of plutocratic capitalism.

At the international level, there have been efforts to create frameworks and agreements that address the challenges posed by global economic inequality and environmental concerns. The Paris Agreement on climate change, for example, represents a collective effort to tackle one of the most pressing global issues, one that is closely linked to the activities of wealthy corporations and nations.

Grassroots movements and civil society organizations have also played a crucial role in resisting plutocratic influences. These movements often focus on raising awareness, mobilizing public opinion, and advocating for change on issues such as income inequality, corporate accountability, and environmental justice. The Occupy Wall Street movement, which spread globally, is an example of a grassroots response to economic inequality and the perceived excesses of plutocratic capitalism.

Another form of resistance comes from the realm of academia and intellectual discourse. Economists, sociologists, and political scientists have critically examined the impacts of plutocratic capitalism, challenging its assumptions and highlighting its shortcomings. This scholarly work has contributed to a broader reevaluation of economic models and theories, considering factors like sustainability, social welfare, and equitable growth.

The digital realm has also emerged as a critical battleground for resistance. Activists and advocacy groups have utilized social media and digital platforms to organize, disseminate information, and challenge the narratives perpetuated by plutocratic interests. These digital tools have enabled new forms of mobilization and engagement, transcending geographical boundaries.

However, resistance to plutocratic capitalism is not without its challenges. The entrenched power and resources of wealthy interests make meaningful change difficult. Additionally, the interconnectedness of the global economy means that actions in one part of the world can have far-reaching effects, complicating efforts to resist or redirect the course of economic policies and practices.

Cultural resistance is another important aspect, where communities and nations strive to preserve their cultural heritage and values against the homogenizing influence of global capitalism. This resistance often involves promoting local traditions, languages, and practices that are at risk of being overshadowed by a dominant global culture.

In conclusion, the global responses and resistance to plutocratic capitalism are diverse and multifaceted. They reflect the complexities of navigating a globalized world where economic power is concentrated in the hands of a few. These responses, whether through policy, grassroots activism, intellectual discourse, or cultural preservation, are crucial in shaping a future that values equity, sustainability, and democratic principles. As the world continues to grapple with the challenges of plutocracy, these forms of resistance play a pivotal role in envisioning and striving for a more equitable global order.

Chapter 6:
Pathways to Reform

Reinforcing Democratic Institutions

In the face of the challenges posed by plutocratic capitalism, reinforcing democratic institutions is a crucial step towards ensuring a more equitable and just society. This section explores the various strategies and reforms needed to strengthen democratic institutions in the United States, ensuring they serve the public interest and resist undue influence from concentrated wealth and power.

The erosion of democratic institutions under the weight of plutocracy is not an irreversible process. Through concerted efforts and strategic reforms, it is possible to revitalize these institutions, making them more resilient and responsive to the needs of all citizens, not just the elite few. Key areas of focus include electoral reform, campaign finance reform, strengthening the rule of law, and enhancing public engagement in the democratic process.

Electoral Reform: One of the primary steps in reinforcing democratic institutions is reforming the electoral system to ensure fair representation and equal access to the political process. This can involve measures such as redistricting reforms to prevent gerrymandering, implementing ranked-choice voting to encourage more diverse candidate selection, and adopting measures to make voting more accessible and secure. Ensuring that elections are free, fair, and transparent is fundamental to the legitimacy of democratic institutions.

Campaign Finance Reform: Addressing the influence of money in politics is crucial for reducing the sway of plutocratic interests. Campaign finance reform might include implementing public financing of elections, setting limits on campaign contributions and expenditures, and increasing transparency around political donations. By reducing the dependence of candidates on wealthy donors, these reforms can help realign political incentives with the broader public interest.

Strengthening the Rule of Law: A robust legal system, free from undue influence, is essential for upholding democratic principles. This involves ensuring the independence and impartiality of the judiciary, combating corruption, and enforcing laws that hold individuals and institutions accountable, regardless of their wealth or status. Strengthening the rule of law also means ensuring that regulatory agencies are effective in their oversight roles, not captured by the industries they are meant to regulate.

Enhancing Public Engagement: Democracy thrives when citizens are informed, engaged, and active in the political process. Efforts to reinforce democratic institutions must therefore include educating the public about their rights and responsibilities, encouraging civic participation, and fostering a culture of open dialogue and debate. This also involves supporting a free and independent press and promoting media literacy to help citizens navigate an increasingly complex information landscape.

Reforming Political Representation: The structure and function of legislative bodies should be reviewed to ensure they represent the diversity of the electorate and are responsive to their needs. This might include measures to increase the representation of traditionally marginalized groups and to ensure that legislative processes are transparent and accountable.

Addressing Economic Inequality: Since economic power translates into political influence, tackling economic inequality is integral to reinforcing democratic institutions. This can involve progressive taxation, social welfare policies, and regulations that ensure fair labor practices and corporate accountability. By addressing the root causes of economic disparity, these measures can help level the playing field and reduce the outsized influence of the wealthy.

International Cooperation: In an increasingly interconnected world, reinforcing democratic institutions also requires international cooperation. Working with other nations and international organizations to promote democratic values, combat corruption, and regulate cross-border economic activities can help create a global environment that supports and upholds democratic principles.

In conclusion, reinforcing democratic institutions in the face of plutocratic capitalism is a multifaceted challenge that requires a comprehensive approach. By implementing reforms in electoral processes, campaign finance, legal systems, and civic engagement, and by addressing underlying economic inequalities, it is possible to create a more robust and resilient democratic framework. These reforms are essential not only for the health of democracy in the United States but also as a model for other nations grappling with similar challenges.

Economic Reforms and Wealth Redistribution

In the quest to counteract the effects of plutocratic capitalism, economic reforms and wealth redistribution are vital steps. This section discusses the necessary economic changes and strategies for redistributing wealth to create a more equitable and sustainable society, thereby addressing the deep-rooted issues of economic inequality and social injustice in the United States.

Economic reforms aimed at wealth redistribution involve a re-evaluation of the existing economic structures and policies to ensure a fairer distribution of wealth and opportunities. Such reforms are not just about alleviating poverty or mitigating inequality; they are about fundamentally reshaping the economic system to align it more closely with democratic principles and social justice.

Progressive Taxation: Implementing a more progressive tax system is a critical aspect of wealth redistribution. This involves higher taxes on the wealthy and large corporations, ensuring they contribute a fairer share to the public coffers. The revenue generated from these taxes can be invested in social programs, education, healthcare, and infrastructure, benefiting society as a whole. Additionally, closing loopholes and addressing offshore tax evasion are essential to ensure the effectiveness of the tax system.

Minimum Wage and Labor Rights: Strengthening labor rights and ensuring a living wage are crucial for reducing economic inequality. Raising the minimum wage to a level that reflects the cost of living and indexing it to inflation can help ensure that working individuals can maintain a decent standard of living. Strengthening unions and collective bargaining rights also play a key role in advocating for workers' rights and fair wages.

Universal Basic Income (UBI): Implementing a UBI is a direct method of wealth redistribution. By providing all citizens with a regular, unconditional sum of money, UBI can help reduce poverty and income inequality, while also providing a safety net for those affected by economic disruptions, such as technological change or global pandemics.

Financial Regulation: Reforming the financial sector to prevent excessive risk-taking and speculative activities is vital. This includes implementing stricter regulations on banking and investment practices, improving transparency, and ensuring that the financial system operates in a way that supports the real economy, not just speculative gains.

Education and Healthcare: Investing in education and healthcare is a long-term strategy for wealth redistribution. Access to quality education can provide individuals with the skills and opportunities needed to improve their economic prospects. Similarly, a robust healthcare system, accessible to all, can prevent medical expenses from becoming a significant source of financial inequality.

Affordable Housing: Addressing the housing crisis, particularly in urban areas, is essential for economic equality. Policies aimed at increasing the supply of affordable housing, regulating the rental market, and providing support for low-income homeowners can help ensure that all citizens have access to safe and affordable housing.

Corporate Accountability and Governance: Reforming corporate governance to prioritize stakeholder interests, including employees and communities, over short-term shareholder profits is crucial. This can involve measures like mandating employee representation on corporate boards, enforcing corporate social responsibility, and regulating executive compensation.

Inclusive Growth Policies: Promoting inclusive growth, where economic benefits are widely shared across society, is essential. This includes supporting small businesses, encouraging local entrepreneurship, and investing in sectors that create jobs and contribute to sustainable development.

Global Cooperation: Addressing wealth inequality and economic reforms is not just a domestic issue; it requires global cooperation. Working with other nations to tackle issues like tax havens, international financial regulation, and trade policies can help create a more equitable global economic system.

In conclusion, economic reforms and wealth redistribution are critical for addressing the challenges posed by plutocratic capitalism. By implementing a combination of progressive taxation, labor rights protection, social investments, and financial regulation, it is possible to create a more equitable economic system. These reforms are not just about redistributing wealth; they are about building a society where economic opportunities and resources are accessible to everyone, paving the way for a more just and sustainable future.

Grassroots Movements and Political Awakening

Grassroots movements and political awakening play a pivotal role in challenging plutocratic capitalism and initiating substantial reforms. This section examines the significance of grassroots activism in driving political and social change, highlighting how collective action at the community level can influence national policies and reshape the political landscape.

Grassroots movements arise from the bottom up, often initiated by ordinary citizens or community groups responding to shared concerns or injustices. These movements are crucial in a democratic society, serving as a counterbalance to the top-down influences of wealthy elites and corporate interests. They can catalyze political awakening, raising awareness about issues that are often overlooked or ignored by mainstream politics.

Mobilizing Public Opinion: Grassroots movements are effective in mobilizing public opinion and drawing attention to specific issues. Through rallies, protests, and public demonstrations, they can highlight social, economic, and political injustices, bringing them to the forefront of public consciousness. This heightened awareness can create pressure on policymakers and elected officials to address the concerns raised by these movements.

Empowering Communities: Grassroots activism empowers communities by giving a voice to those who are often marginalized in the political process. It enables individuals and groups to participate actively in shaping the policies that affect their lives. By organizing at the local level, grassroots movements can foster a sense of agency and collective empowerment, essential for a vibrant democracy.

Influencing Policy: Despite their local or community-based origins, grassroots movements can have a significant impact on national policy. Successful movements can lead to legislative changes, policy reforms, and shifts in political priorities. For example, the Civil Rights Movement in the United States led to landmark legislation that transformed American society, demonstrating the power of grassroots activism to effect change.

Building Networks and Alliances: Grassroots movements often build networks and alliances that extend beyond their immediate community or issue area. By collaborating with other groups, movements can amplify their message, share resources, and create a broader coalition of support. These networks can be particularly effective in challenging the entrenched power of plutocratic interests.

Promoting Political Engagement: Grassroots movements can enhance democratic participation by encouraging people to engage in the political process. This engagement can take various forms, including voting, community organizing, or running for public office. By fostering a more politically active citizenry, grassroots movements can help ensure that the democratic process is more representative and inclusive.

Challenging the Status Quo: Perhaps the most significant role of grassroots movements is in challenging the status quo and advocating for transformative change. These movements can question entrenched power structures, propose alternative visions for society, and advocate for radical reforms that go beyond incremental changes.

Case Studies of Impact: The impact of grassroots movements can be seen in various areas, from environmental activism and labor rights to social justice and anti-corruption campaigns. Movements such as the environmental justice movement, Black Lives Matter, and anti-austerity protests in various countries demonstrate the diverse ways in which grassroots activism can shape the political agenda and drive reform.

The Role of Digital Platforms: In the digital age, social media and online platforms have become vital tools for grassroots movements. They enable rapid dissemination of information, coordination of activities, and mobilization of support across wide geographical areas. Digital activism has expanded the reach and impact of grassroots movements, allowing them to engage with a global audience.

In conclusion, grassroots movements and political awakening are essential components of a healthy democracy, particularly in the context of combating plutocratic capitalism. They provide a means for ordinary citizens to influence the political process, advocate for change, and hold power to account. By fostering political engagement, challenging existing power structures, and advocating for substantive reforms, grassroots movements play a crucial role in shaping a more equitable and just society.

Chapter 7: Envisioning a New Future

Lessons from History

The study of history provides invaluable lessons for understanding and addressing the challenges posed by plutocratic capitalism. This section delves into historical precedents, exploring how past societies have dealt with similar issues of wealth concentration, political corruption, and social inequality. These historical lessons can offer guidance and inspiration for contemporary efforts to reform and revitalize democratic institutions and economic systems.

The Gilded Age and Progressive Era: A pivotal historical period relevant to the current context is the Gilded Age in the United States (late 19th to early 20th century), characterized by rapid industrialization, technological innovation, and stark economic inequality. The era saw the rise of powerful industrialists and financiers, often referred to as "robber barons," whose wealth and influence led to widespread corruption and social injustices. The subsequent Progressive Era brought about significant reforms in response to these challenges, including antitrust laws, labor protections, and the establishment of regulatory bodies. This period demonstrates how public outcry and political activism can lead to meaningful reforms in the face of entrenched wealth and power.

The New Deal: The response to the Great Depression under President Franklin D. Roosevelt in the 1930s offers another critical historical lesson. The New Deal encompassed a series of programs and reforms aimed at providing relief to the unemployed, recovering the economy, and reforming the financial system. These initiatives, including social security, banking regulations, and public works projects, not only addressed immediate economic hardships but also laid the foundation for a more equitable and stable economic system. The New Deal illustrates how government intervention and bold policy initiatives can mitigate economic crises and promote greater social and economic justice.

Scandinavian Social Democracy: The development of social democracy in Scandinavian countries presents a modern example of balancing market economies with robust social welfare systems. These countries have implemented policies that include high levels of taxation, extensive social services, and strong labor rights, leading to relatively low levels of economic inequality and high standards of living. The Scandinavian model shows that it is possible to combine economic efficiency with social equity and underscores the importance of political will and public support in implementing such models.

Decolonization Movements: The decolonization movements in Africa, Asia, and Latin America during the mid-20th century offer lessons on the struggle against economic and political domination. These movements, though primarily focused on political independence, also entailed efforts to reclaim economic resources and assert control over national development paths. They highlight the importance of sovereignty and self-determination in the face of external economic pressures and interests.

The Fall of Communism: The collapse of communist regimes in Eastern Europe and the Soviet Union at the end of the 20th century provides insights into the consequences of extreme centralization of power and the neglect of individual freedoms and market principles. The transition to market economies in these regions underscores the challenges of transforming economic systems and the need for careful balancing of market freedom with social protections.

The Civil Rights Movement: The Civil Rights Movement in the United States during the 1950s and 1960s offers lessons on the power of grassroots mobilization to achieve social and political change. The movement's success in dismantling legal segregation and securing voting rights demonstrates the potential of sustained activism, civil disobedience, and legal challenges to confront systemic injustices.

From these historical lessons, several key themes emerge. First, significant reforms often arise in response to crises or widespread public discontent. Second, effective change requires a combination of grassroots activism, political leadership, and legislative action. Third, balancing economic efficiency with social equity and environmental sustainability is crucial for long-term stability and prosperity. Finally, history teaches that reform is an ongoing process, requiring constant vigilance, adaptation, and participation by all segments of society.

In conclusion, history offers valuable insights and strategies for addressing the challenges of plutocratic capitalism and revitalizing democratic and economic systems. By learning from past successes and failures, contemporary societies can find the inspiration and guidance needed to chart a path toward a more equitable, just, and sustainable future.

A Blueprint for Equitable Democracy

Crafting a blueprint for equitable democracy is crucial in addressing the challenges posed by plutocratic capitalism and in ensuring a fair, just, and inclusive society. This section outlines key principles and strategies to build a more equitable democratic system, drawing on lessons from history, contemporary analyses, and future-oriented thinking.

Foundational Principles: The foundation of an equitable democracy lies in ensuring that all citizens have an equal say in the political process and that their interests are fairly represented. This requires a commitment to fundamental democratic principles such as transparency, accountability, inclusivity, and the rule of law.

Electoral Reforms: A critical starting point is reforming the electoral system to enhance fairness and representation. This includes measures to eliminate gerrymandering, implement campaign finance reform, and ensure access to voting for all citizens. The adoption of proportional representation or ranked-choice voting can also be considered to ensure that election outcomes more accurately reflect the will of the electorate.

Strengthening Institutions: Building strong, independent institutions that can withstand political and economic pressures is essential. This involves bolstering the checks and balances within government, protecting the independence of the judiciary, and ensuring that regulatory bodies are free from corporate influence.

Economic Equity: A more equitable democracy requires addressing economic disparities. Progressive taxation, effective regulation of financial markets, and policies aimed at reducing wealth and income inequality are crucial. Investments in public services such as education, healthcare, and social security contribute to a more level playing field.

Social Justice and Inclusion: Equitable democracy must also address issues of social justice and inclusion. This includes tackling systemic racism, gender inequality, and other forms of discrimination. Policies should aim at not only reducing disparities but also at empowering marginalized communities, ensuring their voices and concerns are represented in the political process.

Civic Engagement and Education: Encouraging active civic engagement and promoting political literacy are vital for a healthy democracy. Educational systems should include comprehensive civics education, teaching individuals about their rights and responsibilities as citizens and the importance of participation in the democratic process.

Environmental Sustainability: Equitable democracy must incorporate environmental sustainability. Policies that balance economic development with environmental protection ensure that the pursuit of prosperity does not come at the cost of ecological degradation or future generations' ability to meet their needs.

Global Perspective: In an interconnected world, a blueprint for equitable democracy also involves engaging with global issues and participating in international efforts to promote democratic values, human rights, and sustainable development.

Technology and Democracy: Addressing the challenges and opportunities presented by technology is essential. Ensuring that digital platforms are used to enhance democratic engagement and do not become tools for misinformation, surveillance, or political manipulation is critical.

Adaptive and Resilient Systems: Finally, equitable democracy requires systems that are adaptable and resilient. This means being open to reform and innovation, learning from experiences, and being prepared to respond to new challenges and opportunities.

Case Studies and Models: Drawing inspiration from successful models around the world, from Scandinavian social democracies to participatory governance models in certain cities and communities, can provide practical ideas for implementation.

In conclusion, a blueprint for equitable democracy involves a multifaceted approach that addresses the political, economic, social, and environmental dimensions of society. It requires a commitment to continuous improvement, openness to learning from global best practices, and engagement from all sectors of society. Building an equitable democracy is an ongoing journey, one that is crucial for the well-being and prosperity of current and future generations.

The Role of Citizens in Shaping Change

The role of citizens is fundamental in shaping change and driving the transition towards an equitable democracy. This section explores the various ways in which individuals and communities can actively participate in the democratic process, influence policy, and contribute to the creation of a society that reflects the values of justice, equality, and inclusivity.

Active Participation in the Democratic Process: Active citizenship is more than just voting in elections. It involves staying informed about political issues, engaging in public discourse, and holding elected officials accountable. Citizens can attend town hall meetings, join local boards and committees, or participate in public demonstrations and advocacy campaigns. By taking an active role in the democratic process, citizens can ensure their voices are heard and their concerns are addressed.

Grassroots Mobilization and Advocacy: Grassroots movements have historically been powerful agents of change. Citizens can initiate or join grassroots campaigns on issues they are passionate about, such as social justice, environmental protection, or economic reforms. These movements often start at a local level but can gain national or even global momentum, influencing policy and societal norms.

Educational and Awareness Initiatives: Educating oneself and others about key issues, democratic processes, and the importance of civic engagement is crucial. This can be achieved through community workshops, discussion groups, and educational campaigns. An informed citizenry is better equipped to make decisions, participate in debates, and contribute to the shaping of public policy.

Utilizing Digital Platforms: In the digital age, citizens have powerful tools at their disposal to influence change. Social media, blogs, and online forums can be used to spread awareness, mobilize support, and engage with a broader audience. Digital platforms can also facilitate online petitions, fundraising for social causes, and the organization of virtual events.

Volunteering and Community Service: Engaging in community service and volunteering for local organizations are direct ways to contribute to societal well-being and foster a sense of community. These activities not only address immediate social needs but also build networks of solidarity and mutual support.

Promoting Inclusive Dialogue and Collaboration: Fostering inclusive dialogue is essential in a diverse society. Citizens can facilitate or participate in discussions that bring together people from different backgrounds and perspectives. These dialogues can lead to a better understanding of shared challenges and the development of collaborative solutions.

Political Leadership and Representation: Citizens can also shape change by seeking political office or supporting candidates who represent their values and interests. Political leadership is not limited to national politics; local councils, school boards, and other community positions are vital platforms for effecting change.

Consumer Choices and Economic Impact: As consumers, citizens have the power to influence corporate practices and market trends. Supporting ethical businesses, advocating for corporate responsibility, and participating in boycotts or buycotts (selectively buying products to support responsible companies) are ways to promote equitable economic practices.

Lifelong Learning and Adaptability: Embracing lifelong learning and staying adaptable in the face of changing societal and global dynamics are essential for effective citizenship. This includes being open to new ideas, adapting to technological advancements, and being prepared to tackle emerging challenges.

Building Alliances and Networks: Change is often more effective when pursued collectively. Building alliances and networks with like-minded individuals, community groups, and organizations can amplify efforts and create a stronger impact. These networks can provide support, resources, and a collective voice for advocating change.

Personal Reflection and Responsibility: Finally, shaping change also involves personal reflection and taking responsibility for one's actions and their impact on society. This includes examining personal beliefs and biases, making ethical decisions, and considering the broader implications of one's choices.

In conclusion, the role of citizens in shaping change is multifaceted and indispensable. Through active participation, grassroots mobilization, education, digital engagement, and personal responsibility, citizens can drive the transition towards a more equitable and democratic society. It is the collective effort and commitment of individuals that ultimately shapes the course of a nation and its values.